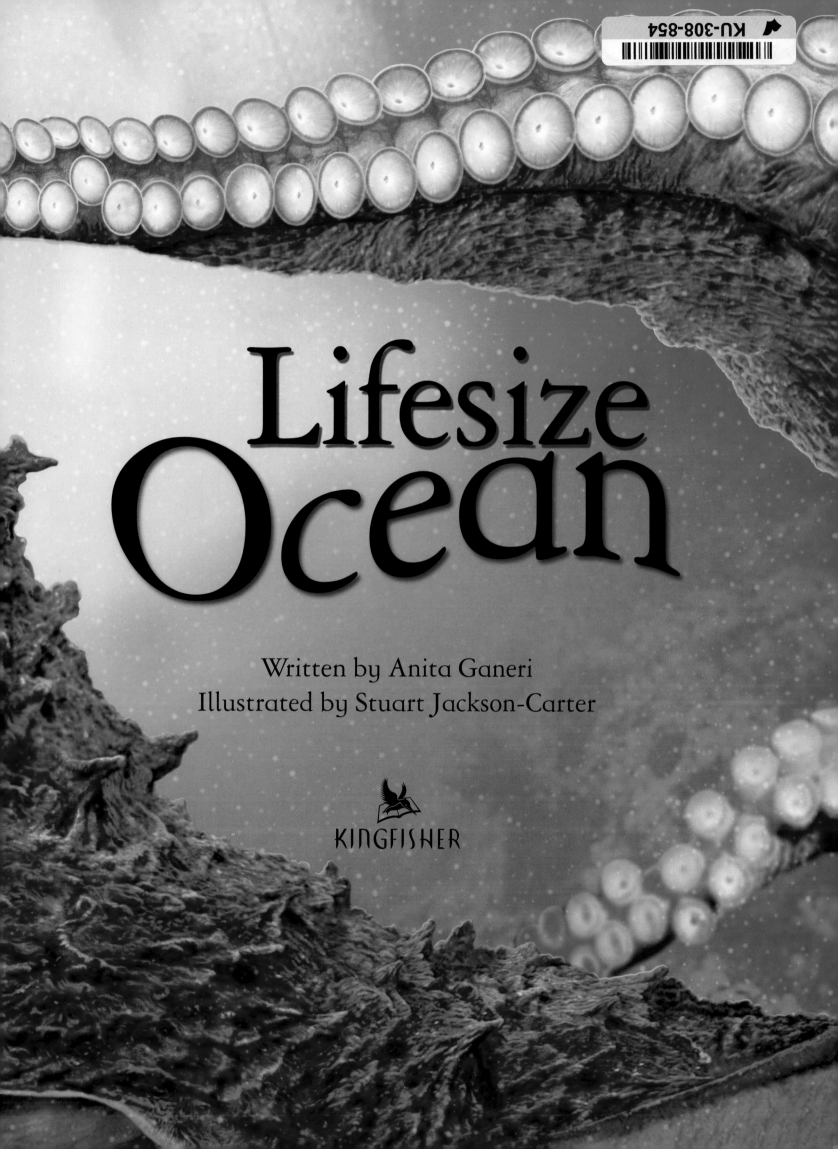

Lifesize Ocean

Written by Anita Ganeri

Illustrated by Stuart Jackson-Carter

KINGFISHER

KINGFISHER

First published 2014 by Kingfisher
an imprint of Macmillan Children's Books
a division of Macmillan Publishers Limited
20 New Wharf Road, London N1 9RR
Basingstoke and Oxford
Associated companies throughout the world
www.panmacmillan.com

Consultant: Steve Savage
Editor: Clare Hibbert
Design and styling: Maj Jackson-Carter
Cover design: Mike Davis

ISBN 978-0-7534-3634-9

1 3 5 7 9 8 6 4 2

1TR/0114/WKT/UG/128MA

A CIP catalogue record for this book is available from the British Library.

Printed in China

Contents

4   Copepods

6   Pygmy seahorses

8   Red skunk cleaner shrimps

10 Blue-ringed octopuses

12 Black devil anglerfish

14 Long-spined porcupine fish

16 Sea otters

18 Green sea turtle

20 Purple-striped jellyfish

22 Great hammerhead shark

24 North Pacific giant octopus

26 Blue whale

28 Animal facts

32 Saving ocean animals

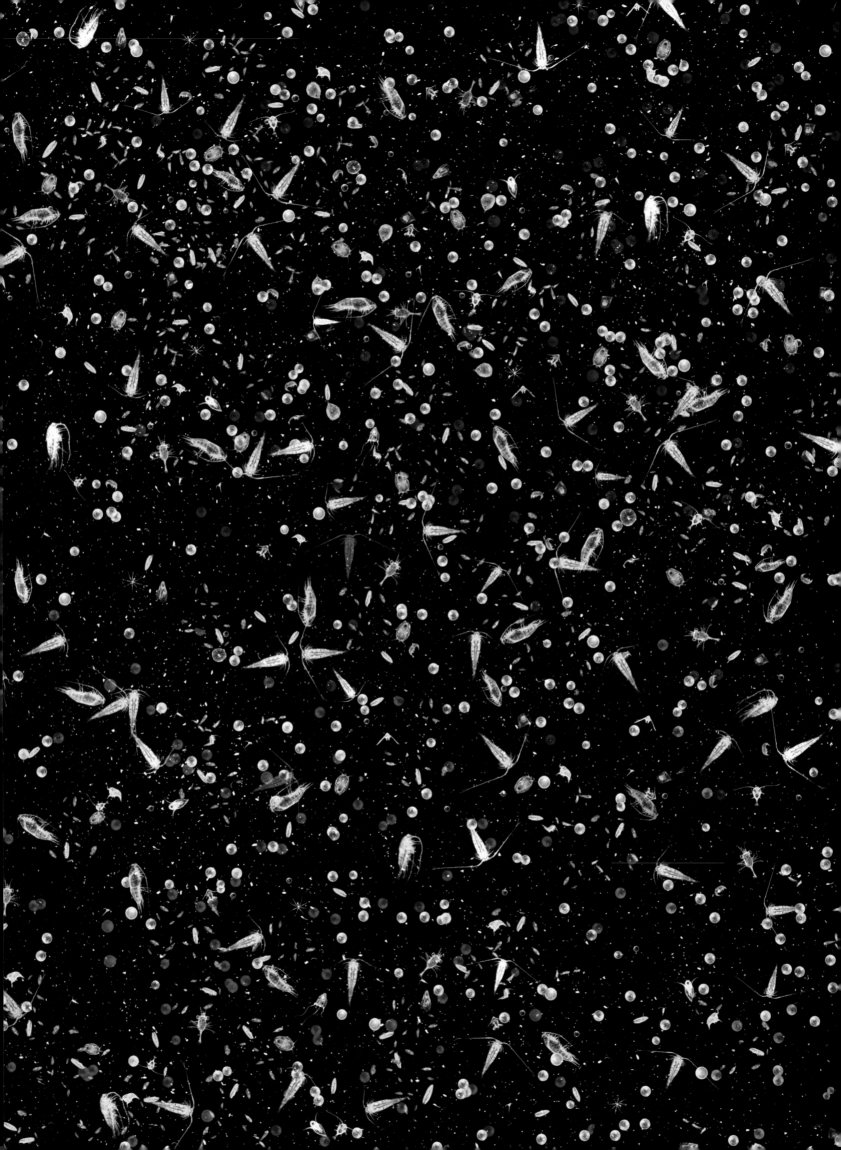

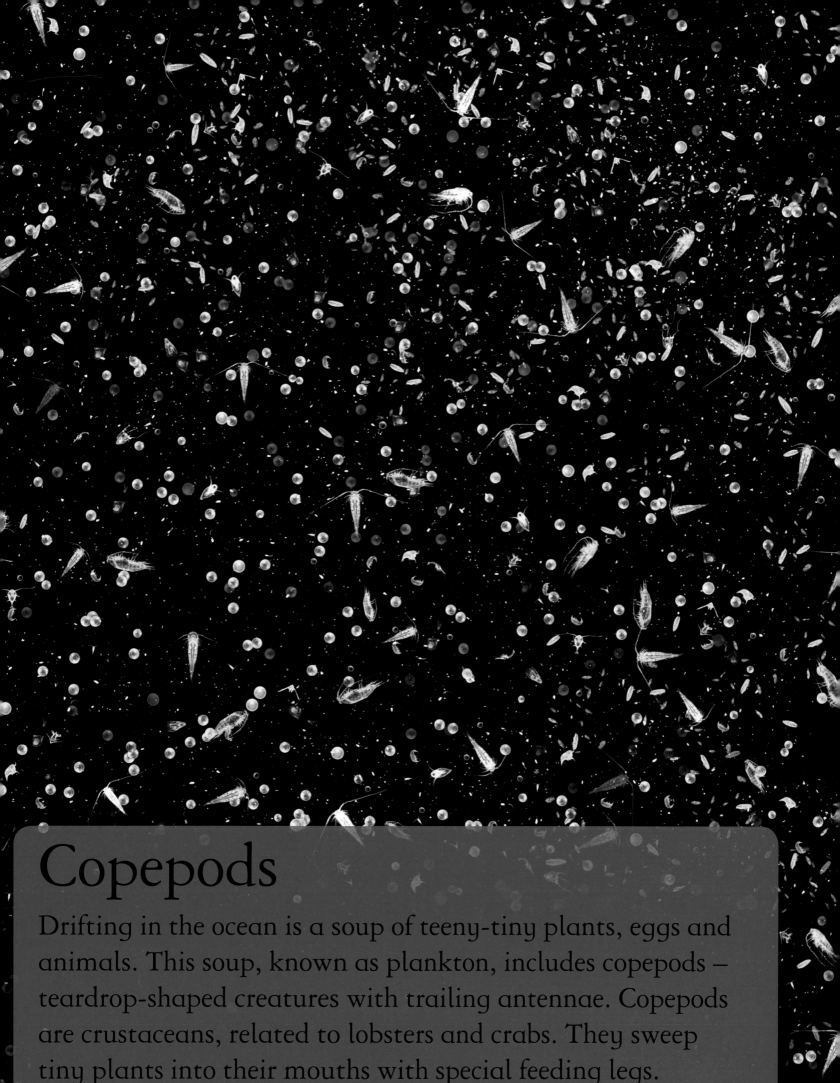

Copepods

Drifting in the ocean is a soup of teeny-tiny plants, eggs and animals. This soup, known as plankton, includes copepods – teardrop-shaped creatures with trailing antennae. Copepods are crustaceans, related to lobsters and crabs. They sweep tiny plants into their mouths with special feeding legs.

Pygmy seahorses

How many pygmy seahorses are in this picture? Look carefully – they are tricky to spot! Not only are these amazing animals small, they are also brilliantly camouflaged. Pygmy seahorses only live on sea fans, a type of coral. They match the coral perfectly, right down to their lumps and bumps.

Turn to page 32 to check how many seahorses are in the picture.

Red skunk cleaner shrimps

A moray eel stops for a welcome clean. This usually ferocious fish stays quite still as a team of red skunk cleaner shrimps sets to work. They scurry all over its body, picking parasites and dead scales off its skin and gills. They even venture inside the eel's mouth, to nibble bits of leftover food from its sharp teeth!

Blue-ringed octopuses

Two blue-ringed octopuses prowl the reef, on the lookout for crabs and fish. These delicate creatures are small and usually shy. But they are also some of the deadliest animals in the ocean, capable of killing a human in minutes, with a single, venomous bite.

Black devil anglerfish

In the dark, deep sea, a female anglerfish lurks. She has a long fin, like a fishing rod, with a glowing blob of light at the end. When prey comes close, attracted by the light, her gaping mouth snaps shut. This anglerfish must nourish both herself and her much smaller mate, who clings to her belly by his teeth.

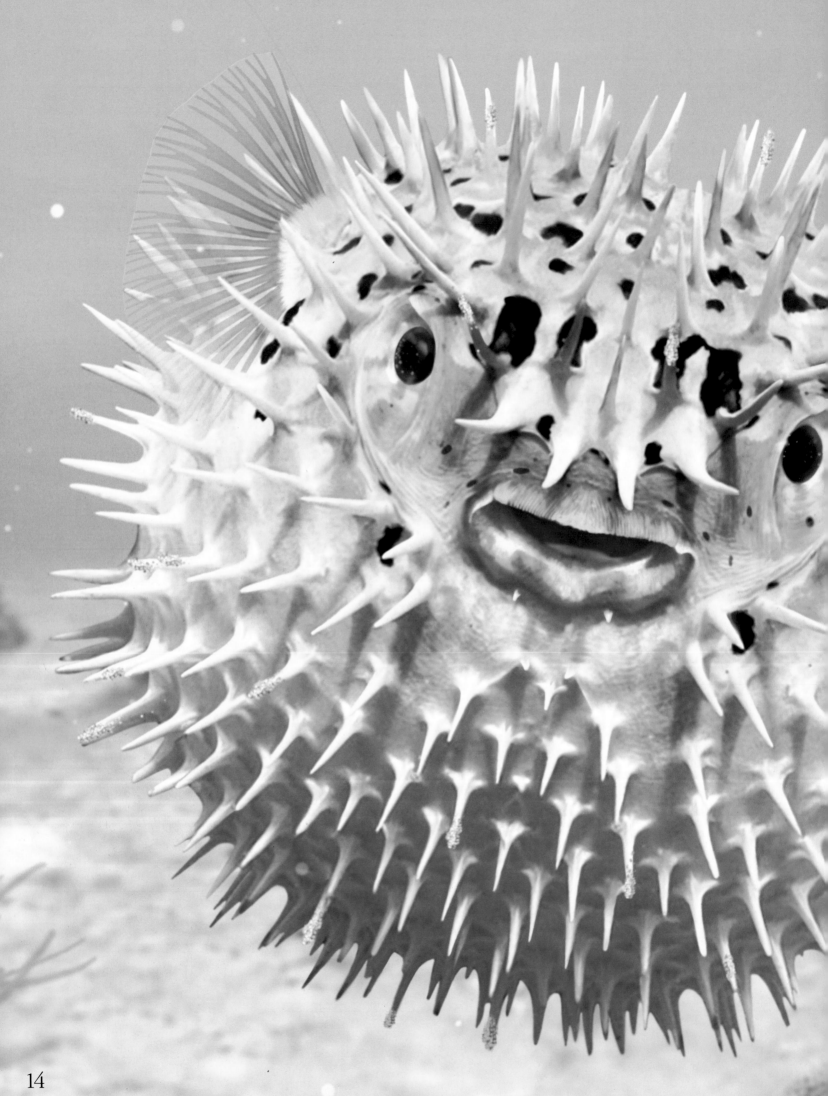

Long-spined porcupine fish

Faced with a hungry predator, a porcupine fish gulps in water and blows itself up to twice its usual size. The long, sharp spines on its body stick up, making it too big and prickly a mouthful for any attacker. Once the danger has passed, the fish shrinks back to normal, its spines flat against its skin.

Sea otters

A sea otter mum and her pup doze in the water, wrapped in strands of seaweed to stop them drifting away. When she wakes, the mother dives for mussels, clams and sea urchins. She lies on her back and smashes the shellfish against a rock balanced on her chest to get at the meat inside.

Green sea turtle

Using its front flippers as paddles, a green sea turtle powers through the water, occasionally surfacing to breathe. It spends most of its life at sea but females come ashore to lay their eggs. When the babies hatch, they must dash to the sea or risk being eaten by hungry gulls and ghost crabs.

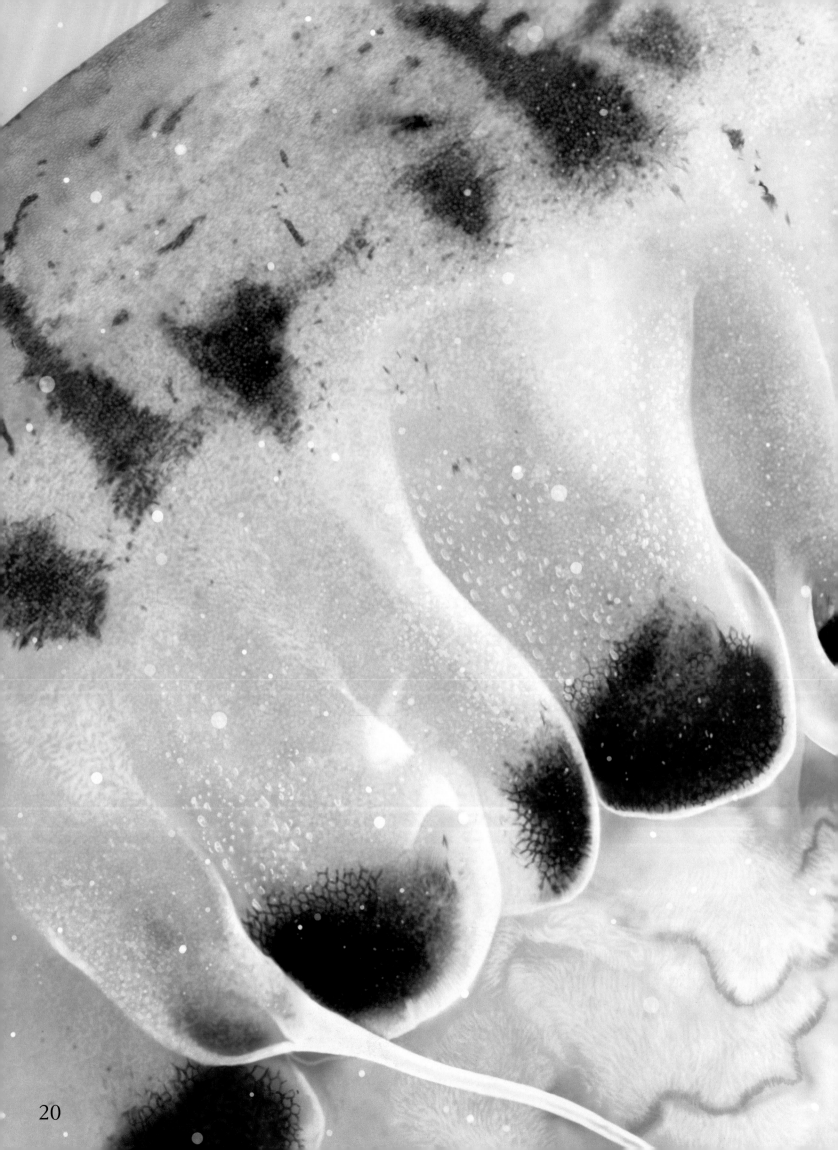

Purple-striped jellyfish

With its bright stripes, this giant jellyfish is a striking sight – but it is also armed and dangerous! It trails long tentacles, covered in stinging cells. They stun or kill any copepods or other prey that brush past them, and then the jellyfish can pull its meal into its mouth.

Great hammerhead shark

A great hammerhead scans the water for stingrays, its favourite food. The shark's odd, hammer-shaped head has special sensors that pick up electrical signals from a ray buried in the sand. The shark can use the side of its head to pin down its prey so it can't escape. Then the hunter bites off big chunks of the ray's flesh.

North Pacific giant octopus

As night falls, a North Pacific giant octopus leaves its den to go hunting. Each of its eight arms is as long as a human diver and studded with suckers. The octopus stalks or chases its prey. Its beak-like mouth can bite open crab or mollusc shells, or drill a hole for sucking out the insides.

26

Blue whale

Everything about a blue whale is ENORMOUS, from eyeballs as big as grapefruits to a heart the size of a small car. Its favourite food are tiny, shrimp-like creatures called krill. The whale gulps in a massive mouthful of water, sieves out all the krill, squirts out the water and then swallows the krill.

Animal facts

Most copepods have a single, bright red eye on their head.

Like all octopuses, the blue-ringed octopus has three hearts and blue blood.

Red skunk cleaner shrimp

UNDER THREAT

Habitat: Coral reefs in the Indian and Pacific Oceans

Length: Up to 6cm

Weight: Not known

Diet: Parasites, dead skin and fungus

Average lifespan: 3–5 years

Amazing fact: The shrimps' bright colours make them easy to spot at their cleaning stations. They also wave their antennae and do a special dance to attract passing fish.

Blue-ringed octopus

Habitat: Reefs and rock pools around Australia and the western Pacific Ocean

Length of body: 5cm

Length of tentacles: 7–7.5cm

Weight: Around 26kg

Diet: Crabs, fish and molluscs

Average lifespan: 2 years

Amazing fact: The octopus has a pattern of 50 to 60 rings on its body. When it is alarmed, the rings glow bright blue, warning that the octopus might bite.

Copepod

UNDER THREAT

Habitat: Oceans around the world

Length: 1–5mm

Weight: Less than 1mg

Diet: Phytoplankton (tiny plants) and zooplankton (tiny animals)

Average lifespan: Less than a year

Amazing fact: Copepods use their long antennae to detect food and enemies. They can tell which is which by sensing the way water flows around their bodies.

The shrimp is named after the white stripe down its back, like a skunk's.

Pygmy seahorses curl their tails around sea fans to avoid being swept away.

Pygmy seahorse

UNDER THREAT

Habitat: Coral reefs in the western Pacific Ocean

Length: Up to 2cm

Weight: Not known

Diet: Tiny shrimps and other crustaceans

Average lifespan: 12–18 months

Amazing fact: Male seahorses have babies. The male carries the eggs in a pouch on his front until they hatch. Then up to 30 tiny babies shoot out and swim away.

UNDER THREAT

Animals are under threat if their numbers are falling and they risk becoming extinct (dying out forever). Or they may be under threat because their habitat is disappearing.

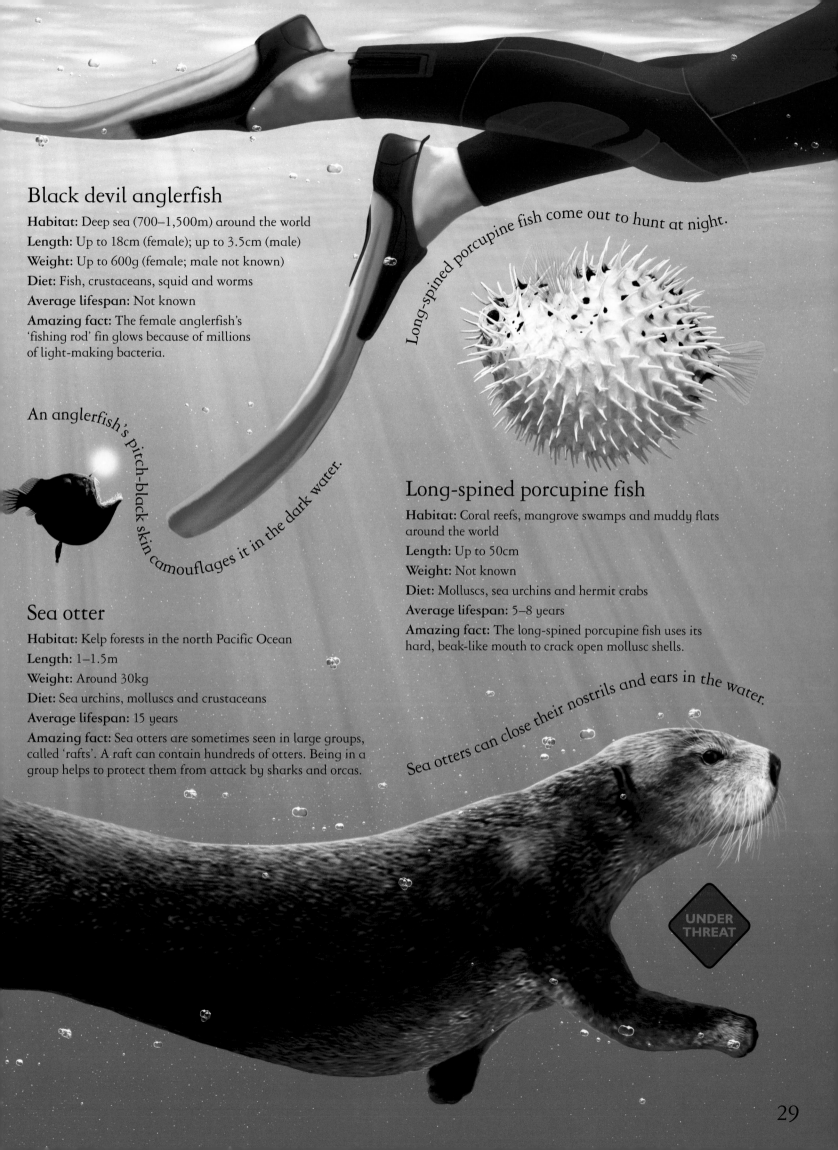

Black devil anglerfish

Habitat: Deep sea (700–1,500m) around the world

Length: Up to 18cm (female); up to 3.5cm (male)

Weight: Up to 600g (female; male not known)

Diet: Fish, crustaceans, squid and worms

Average lifespan: Not known

Amazing fact: The female anglerfish's 'fishing rod' fin glows because of millions of light-making bacteria.

An anglerfish's pitch-black skin camouflages it in the dark water.

Long-spined porcupine fish come out to hunt at night.

Long-spined porcupine fish

Habitat: Coral reefs, mangrove swamps and muddy flats around the world

Length: Up to 50cm

Weight: Not known

Diet: Molluscs, sea urchins and hermit crabs

Average lifespan: 5–8 years

Amazing fact: The long-spined porcupine fish uses its hard, beak-like mouth to crack open mollusc shells.

Sea otter

Habitat: Kelp forests in the north Pacific Ocean

Length: 1–1.5m

Weight: Around 30kg

Diet: Sea urchins, molluscs and crustaceans

Average lifespan: 15 years

Amazing fact: Sea otters are sometimes seen in large groups, called 'rafts'. A raft can contain hundreds of otters. Being in a group helps to protect them from attack by sharks and orcas.

Sea otters can close their nostrils and ears in the water.

UNDER THREAT

Green sea turtles have green fat underneath their shells.

Green sea turtle

Habitat: Tropical oceans around the world

Length: Up to 1.5m

Weight: Around 130kg

Diet: Algae and seagrass

Average lifespan: 80 years

Amazing fact: Green sea turtles travel long distances to breed. Some swim more than 2,000km from Brazil to tiny Ascension Island in the middle of the Atlantic Ocean.

UNDER THREAT

Purple-striped jellyfish

Habitat: Open waters off the Californian coast, Pacific Ocean

Diameter of bell (body): Up to 1m

Length of tentacles: Up to 5m

Weight: Not known

Diet: Copepods, jellyfish and fish eggs

Average lifespan: Not known

Amazing fact: Young purple-striped jellyfish don't have purple stripes. They have pale pink bells and long, dark red tentacles. They change colour as they get older.

Some crabs live inside purple-striped jellyfish and feed on harmful parasites.

Blue whales have super-loud voices! They can hear each other from 1,600km away – unless other sounds, such as boat engines, get in the way.

Hammerheads give birth to litters of up to 40 pups.

North Pacific giant octopus

Habitat: Coastal areas of the north Pacific Ocean

Armspan: Up to 5m

Weight: Up to 50kg

Diet: Crustaceans, molluscs and small fish

Average lifespan: 3–5 years

Amazing fact: When an octopus is alarmed or disturbed, it can activate special cells in its skin and change colour from reddish-brown to white or red.

Female giant octopuses lay strings of 20,000 to 100,000 eggs.

Great hammerhead shark

UNDER THREAT

Habitat: Open and coastal waters around the world

Length: Up to 6m

Weight: Up to 450kg

Diet: Stingrays and other fish, squid and octopuses

Average lifespan: 20–30 years

Amazing fact: Great hammerheads' heads are 60 to 90cm wide. When hunting at dawn and dusk, they swing their heads to and fro to pick up signals from their prey.

Blue whale

UNDER THREAT

Habitat: Oceans around the world (except the Arctic)

Length: Up to 30m

Weight: Up to 200 tonnes

Diet: Krill

Average lifespan: 80–90 years

Amazing fact: Blue whales give birth to babies that are already 7m long and weigh more than 2 tonnes. By drinking its mother's rich milk, a baby whale can double its weight in a week.

Saving ocean animals

All over the world, oceans and their wildlife are in danger from pollution, oil and gas drilling, global warming and overfishing. Scientists, conservation groups and governments are working hard to learn more about the oceans so that they can find better ways of looking after them. One plan is to turn parts of the ocean into parks where animals and plants are protected. The Great Barrier Reef off the coast of Australia is already a marine park.

Why are green sea turtles in danger?

Many are caught for their meat and eggs.

Others die after swallowing plastic.

Thousands more get tangled in fishing nets, and drown.

Five groups working to save ocean animals:

Greenpeace works to protect the environment. It is campaigning for more marine parks, and less harmful ways of fishing. www.greenpeace.org

The Hebridean Whale and Dolphin Trust is dedicated to the conservation of whales, dolphins and porpoises off the west coast of Scotland. www.whaledolphintrust.org

The Marine Conservation Society campaigns to protect oceans, coastlines and their wildlife. Its Cool Seas Roadshow visits schools around the UK. www.mcsuk.org

The Sea Turtle Conservancy was set up to stop sea turtles becoming extinct. It tracks individual turtles by satellite. www.conserveturtles.org

The Shark Trust carries out projects to protect sharks and their habitats. Its site has a Pups' Activity Zone geared towards young people. www.sharktrust.org

Answer: There are 16 pygmy seahorses in the picture on pages 6 and 7.